W0006308

TO THE BOYS *on the* OTHER SIDE

Neil Janney

ISBN: 1481808400
ISBN-13: 9781481808408

PREFACE

My two great-grandfathers, Jasper Smith and Ellwood Janney, served in the Eighteenth Michigan Infantry during the American Civil War. Knowing very little about their experiences, I decided to research and retrace the Eighteenth Michigan's war experiences. The unit was first assigned in 1862 to Lexington, Kentucky, where it skirmished and then to Nashville, Tennessee. There it was assigned provost duties, sort of the military police. No dramatic combat there either.

Then, in 1864, it was transferred to Decatur, Alabama, way down south across the Tennessee River. October 1864 was a critical time. In September after defeating John Bell Hood's army, William Tecumseh Sherman's army occupied Atlanta, Georgia. Desperate to drive Sherman out of Georgia, the Confederacy decided to march Hood's army to Tennessee and retake Nashville. The Confederate leadership believed that the Union forces under General Thomas would not be able to withstand Hood, who had at least thirty-five thousand troops, maybe more. This would then draw Sherman's army into Tennessee and out of Georgia. A Confederate victory in Tennessee could well cause President Abraham Lincoln to lose the presidential election that was looming in November. The North was war weary after four years of fighting and unbelievable deaths. Lincoln's former top general, George McClellan, was running against him and wanted to negotiate an end to the war. But this would mean a continuation of slavery, either in a new Confederate nation or in a reunited United States that still supported slavery.

Hood had to cross the Tennessee River. Union generals were frantically trying to locate him, but his entire army had disappeared. At Decatur, Alabama, a pontoon bridge crossed the Tennessee River. On the south shore stood a little "fort."

It was nothing more than a former bank building, built of stone blocks, with its back to the river; its front was defended by a semi-circle of earth embankments and trenches. The fort was occupied by 1,800 Union troops, which included the Eighteenth Michigan, Ohio, and Indiana troops. Recent reinforcements also included the newly formed Fourteenth US Colored—former slaves now armed and dressed in Union blue uniforms. In a twist of fate, the fort was temporarily commanded by the Eighteenth Michigan commander, Colonel Doolittle, a former banker. He replaced a general who had resigned, saying he could not defend the bridge with these forces that were equipped with worn-out cannons and old muzzle-loading rifles.

On October 26th, 1864, just weeks before the presidential election, the suspense of Hood's location was broken when he made a surprise attack on the little Decatur fortification. There, Ellwood and Jasper engaged in their first major battle. The world little noted and overlooked this battle, even as it critically helped President Lincoln avoid defeat in the election. So we join Jasper and Ellwood to creatively tell their story.

TABLE OF CONTENTS

EIGHTEENTH MICHIGAN INFANTRY, NIGGER THIEVERY REGIMENT

The Eighteenth Michigan Infantry was first assigned to Kentucky. Oddly, a great many of the men were or had been Quakers—pacifists who refused to fight in the Revolutionary War. But, staunch abolitionist beliefs prevailed over peaceful means. Many answered the call of Lincoln for troops.

They were first sent to Kentucky. There hadn't been much fighting in Kentucky, but the Eighteenth gained a reputation for helping escaped slaves flee to the safety of Ohio, just across the river from their encampment. Technically an escaped slave was property and should be returned to the owner—especially if the owner lived in Kentucky, which remained in the Union. The idea of returning a man to slavery did not sit well, since most of the regiment enlisted to fight slavery, not save the Union. The sheriff would show up with a writ of replevin (a legal remedy usually used by farmers to recover stolen livestock).

In one instance, the Eighteenth soldiers welcomed a sheriff to look around for the missing slave, while they held his horse. Once the sheriff dismounted, someone smacked the horse. It reared and ran, with soldiers and the sheriff in pursuit. By the time the horse was returned, the escaped slave fled to another location—across the Ohio, up to Detroit, and then to permanent freedom in Canada.

A Kentucky Union officer lost many of his slaves, courtesy of his fellow Michigan regiment. In great anger he had written to President Lincoln, pointing out that he was a loyal Union officer (and lawyer), that slavery was legal in Kentucky since the state had not seceded, and that he had given up a great deal of revenue by serving in the Union army. He also wrote that Lincoln should discipline this damned Eighteenth Michigan Infantry—in his words, this "Nigger Thievery Regiment." Lincoln never responded. So, to the delight of the regiment, it adopted this name, the Nigger Thievery Regiment. But then came orders, transferring them first to Nashville, then to this godforsaken place way down south in Decatur, Alabama, on the south bank of the Tennessee River. The regiment dropped the name.

Way Down South in Alabama

"There will be no surrender, gentlemen. That is all, dismissed." With those words, General Granger and Colonel Doolittle turned and stared out the window, while the officers filed down the stairs from the second floor of the fort headquarters. It was not really a fort, just a semicircle of trenches and earth works surrounding a large two-story building that backed up against the Tennessee River. It was the only building left standing in the town of Decatur, Alabama. All of the surrounding trees had been cut down, and all the other buildings had been destroyed. Anyone approaching them could be seen and shot at with a clear line of fire. It was a spacious, well-lit building with stone walls, wooden floors, and large, Grecian style front pillars. The south windows looked out on the trenches and the area beyond, desolate of any trees or bushes. From the north windows, the Tennessee River flowed just a few hundred yards away. A narrow pontoon bridge reached across the Tennessee to the north, beckoning the men to leave this little fort stuck in the eye of the Confederacy. Rail traffic was visible on the north side with frequent eastbound trains, whistling and huffing with men, food, and ammunition headed to Sherman's forces in Georgia.

The building had been a bank before the war, and Ellwood left the building somewhat reluctantly—it gave him a feeling of security that the trenches surrounding the building lacked. It was hard to keep a clean uniform in the dirt outside, and he had just been promoted from sergeant to an officer. He was conscious of his new status as acting commander of Company A of the Eighteenth Michigan Infantry. He wanted to look and do well. It was late October in 1864, and the oppressive heat had fled.

With both the Gettysburg and Vicksburg victories now over a year old, it was inconceivable to Ellwood that the war was not over. He had enlisted in 1862 at Hillsdale, Michigan, shortly after the start of the rebellion of the southern states. Expecting to serve about four months, it was now 1864. His unit, the Eighteenth Michigan Infantry, had survived so far without major casualties, although it had seen combat in the form of skirmishes. In his opinion, the Eighteenth appeared to be deliberately positioned to be in harm's way in Alabama. Alabama! It might as well have been other side of the world. He had never been south of Toledo, Ohio, before the war started. It was just inconceivable that, at this late date, death or capture looked so imminent. He worked hard at thinking of a distraction, so he would not show his anxiety when he told the company the news.

Shall Not Pass

According to General Granger, it appeared that General Hood's entire army had surrounded this fort, which defended the bridge running north across the Tennessee River. Hood's mission was to get across the river and march onto Nashville to the north. With the nation's presidential election looming, the Rebels figured the capture of Nashville—even as Sherman marched through Georgia—would cause so much dismay in the North that it would cause the defeat of Lincoln. Lincoln's ex-general of the Union Army, McClellan, was running on a promise to negotiate a settlement with the South and end the war. His promise, however, would allow slavery to continue in the Confederacy and split the nation. All the sacrifice would have been in vain. Yet the bridge was defended by a scant two thousand Union troops, vastly inferior to Hood's army, which the general estimated at thirty-five thousand.

Ellwood thought of his family farm in southern Michigan and hoped his brother and father were running it ok. Ellwood was a teetotaler, and their frequent whiskey capers especially worried him. It would be cold and frosty there with the dry, standing, light-brown corn and the orange squash. The black walnuts would be dark green and falling off the trees. He wondered why they were not called "green walnuts" because that was the color of the walnuts' outer skin. His thoughts jolted back to Decatur, Alabama. The Fourteenth US Colored Regiment's commanding officer, a colonel he did not know, was walking just ahead. All of the colored troops had white officers. Ellwood reflected on the use of "colored" to describe the unit. The soldiers, once slaves, had been only recently freed and organized in Tennessee. He wondered if it would have added a little sting for the South if the army had called them the "Fourteenth US Tennessee." Ellwood pondered on the use of "white" to describe anyone who wasn't a Negro, as his skin was more olive than white, but his fixation on words was broken by the music coming from the band in Confederate lines.

Grapes of Wrath

Ellwood reflected on the previous day. He had been in the headquarters building, working on a few inventory reports, for he had just taken over command of his company and had to sign for all the equipment. But he was not rushed. No one expected much to happen. Colonel C.C. Doolittle, commander of the 18th, had briefed them at a staff meeting that Hood was somewhere south of Chattanooga but had dropped out of sight. Everyone was supposed to be vigilant, but it was quiet. A clock ticked with the swing of a pendulum. And the Indiana volunteers sent out a scouting detail.

Much to everyone's dismay, General Granger ordered the troops to man battle positions, night and day, in the trenches. The troops were weary, bored, and irritable. A West Pointer, General Granger had replaced General Stevens, who was a politician prior to the war. General Stevens was laid back and a regular fellow. He showed concern about the troops, and life had been pretty easy under him. Now they drilled frequently and had been forced to be ready every hour of the day and night. It seemed so ridiculous to keep these men in the trenches, days on end, when no enemy was in sight. Even Colonel Doolittle gave them no respite, even though General Granger had temporarily left. Ellwood was dismayed at Colonel Doolittle's new, tough manner. He had been the family banker back in Michigan—at home in this bank, he thought.

Ellwood liked the architecture of the building—tall, wide windows of wavy glass let in ample light. The floor panels were smooth. He leaned back in the swivel chair and studied the ceiling. At the top, a fancy design embedded in plaster framed the perimeter. Tall candles stood in the great chandeliers. Ellwood thought the building stamped everyone working in it with the words "You are important." Otherwise you would not be working here. He wished he had a cigar to smoke.

Then, a few distant "pop pops" tried to interrupt the serenity of it. Ellwood put his feet down and brought his mind back to the task at hand. He dipped a feather quill in the black ink and entered another line—*knapsacks*. He paused to admire his handwriting. Next he etched a number with the quill in the quantity column. Distinct shouting and gunfire clearly came from just beyond the trench lines. He went to the window. The glass made wavy figures of horses galloping full speed towards the fort. The horses of the Hoosier Cavalry appeared to be suspended in the air with front legs extended full forward and back legs extended full back. Several horses bore empty saddles. Ellwood wondered if it were true that "Hoosiers" was the nickname for Indianians because they always asked, "Whoosheare?" when someone knocked on their door.

"Get ready to give 'em grape!'" shouted a voice from somewhere below. Still watching from the window, Ellwood's mind astonishingly flitted briefly to Michigan.

Up in Michigan Father had planted a good, long row of grapes from plants that had carefully been wrapped in wet rags and carried all the way from the family homestead in Newton, Pennsylvania. When ripe, the dark dark-purple ovals hung heavily on the vine. Each grape tasted like a royal snack. The skins were thick, and a good squeeze would pop the inside fruit right into your mouth. They were so tasty and refreshing, and they were also plentiful and free. Then his mind snapped back to the scene below.

His body stiffened. The dust rolled up from the hundreds—no, a thousand, maybe more—of shouting and shooting figures charging the trenches that surrounded the fort. Shouting erupted everywhere from inside the trenches. The bugler tried to play something, but it wasn't coming out too well. From everywhere in the trenches, muskets pointed outwards by the recently bored and bitter men, who were stiffly cramped from waiting. Now standing they fired. Puffs of smoke emitted from their rifles.

It occurred to Ellwood he should not be standing in the window in full view, but from his second-story level he could see everything. He could not stop looking. The Hoosiers and their horses were now safe behind the lines, but this approaching wave of men was making a strange sound. So this was the Rebel yell? He had never heard it. It sounded bird like—an attack of crazed birds.

Closer they came. It looked clear that they would run right over the top of the trenches. Since he had been made an officer, Ellwood no longer carried a rifle. He had a saber and a pistol. He felt absolutely naked without his rifle. Here the enemy came, and he was not really good with a pistol. He could still not move away from the window. He put his hand on the saber, then changed his mind, and put his hand on the pistol grip. At least it was something. But it was only good for about fifty feet and would be futile from the bank window, even if he had been a crack shot.

The shrieking men were now shooting right at the trenches, rolled up like a big wave about to crash over a helpless pier, when the command went out: "GIVE 'EM THE GRAPE! FIRE AT WILL!"

The fortifications were well designed. General Dodge, the railway engineer, had personally inspected and made certain changes. The unit's cannons were hand-me-downs, worn out in other battles but well positioned. Inaccurate at long range but loaded with grape shot that, at such close range, it mattered not that the cannon barrels were worn. The "grapes" would explode in a wide, deadly, and devastating spray pattern. The small balls of lead were much deadlier than the large cannon ball.

Ellwood looked down. The noise must have been deafening but seemed barely audible to him. The rushing wave of men just stopped as if hitting some monstrous blast of air, which blew them backwards. The entire front of the line just crumpled. Ellwood wasn't sure, but it looked like the tops of some of the men went backwards. And then the lower part of their bodies marched forward without the top part. Flashes and smoke from the trenches hit those still standing as another round of grape left the vine.

"GET BACK, GET DOWN, LIEUTENANT!" Ellwood stepped back, pulled down by a hand gripping his shoulder. It was Colonel Doolittle.

"My God, there are thousands of them, Colonel!!"

"Get off a telegram to Huntsville. Tell them we are under attack by a large force and that we cut down the first charge." The colonel looked out cautiously from the edge of the window.

"Get a message to Huntsville!" Ellwood ran down the steps to the telegraph room and shouted to the operator.

"Hood's army is here, and we stopped 'em so far." Ellwood watched as the operator calmly sat there and began exercising his finger on the key. It made a tapping sound. Ellwood stared. The man's hand was so steady. He could have been sending a routine inventory report. *How does he do that?* thought Ellwood. He looked down at his hand now holding the pistol, which he did not remember pulling from the holster. It was shaking quite visibly.

Not wanting anyone to see his shaking hand, he ran out the door and down into the trenches where his company fired over the top. "IT'S THE WHOLE GODDAMN ARMY—THEY—THEY ARE—MANGLED, KEEP...FIRING!" Corporal Jasper Smith looked shocked. Ellwood, a Quaker, never used profanity like that. Jasper never paused in his firing, tearing the paper-gunpowder pouch with his teeth. He pushed down the powder, a wad, and ball with his ramrod—an old worn-out musket that fired but one shot. Then Jasper repeated the routine.

"Give 'em the grape again!!" shouted a voice. Then everything was quiet, except for moaning and distant, bugle-retreat sounds.

Ellwood now reflected on the sight he had seen and was amazed. He knew morally he should feel horror and sympathy for the terrible deaths of so many brave men. But it had been so thrilling, and the image of the grape on these men—well—he had learned to despise the Rebel cause so much that it gave him great pleasure. He flushed with the shame of such thoughts but could not help the almost spiritual feeling it gave him. So this was war. He felt awe, pure awe. War was not to be loathed as he had been taught. Instead it seemed, well, so, so rewarding. After all, they were killing for a good cause, he told himself. Still he wished he felt some remorse, not glee.

AND THE BAND PLAYED ON

October 27, 1864, was the second day of fighting. Each Confederate rush had been repulsed, with more Confederate casualties and hardly any to the entrenched Union troops. The dead simply disappeared. The other side would holler, "Burial detail!" and the Union troops would oblige. Ellwood estimated maybe five hundred to one thousand dead on the other side. He knew about fifty Union soldiers were dead mostly from the Indiana 102nd. Their bodies had been whisked away too.

The firing from the Confederate side stopped, replaced by band music. This did not seem unusual. Music was part of the daily life and every unit had a functioning band drawn from the talent available. Everyone paused to listen to a marching song "The Bonnie Blue Flag." Then came one aimed at Union soldiers so far from their northern homes – "Weeping Sad and Lonely." *That hits hard,* Ellwood thought. This war has just been too long. Jasper, his compatriot and friend since forever, and Ellwood had volunteered together, answering the call of President Lincoln for troops. Both expected the war to take about four months at the most. Now two years, going on three, seemed like ten, and rather than going home to march in a victory parade, things looked pretty grim. The music was an interruption, a rather pleasant break from the shooting. Ellwood had no ability to play or sing. He was like General Grant, who supposedly knew two tunes—one was "Yankee Doodle Dandy" and the other wasn't. Still Ellwood enjoyed and appreciated good music.

"Put them on the roof," ordered General Granger, who now stood behind Ellwood.

"Sir?" Elwood was perplexed and stood silently. Such an order would expose the band—many of his friends—to direct fire from the Confederate lines.

"Put the band on the roof and answer the music—now!" ordered the General again. Ellwood still stood silently, looking at the General whose face was reddening.

"Band—up on the roof, double time," bellowed a nearby major. The band members lost no time and ran up ladders that were placed there for the lookouts and sharp shooters. Normally the band might have questioned the order and even argued. But the general was a regular army officer, and they had heard him give the order. His voice left no room for hesitation.

"Yankee Doodle" soon rang out to the cheers of the Union troops below in the trenches. The band stopped, and the Rebel band answered with "When Johnny Comes Marching Home." The Rebel yell sounded at the conclusion.

"Play 'John's Brown Body!'" someone shouted from the Union trenches. The band played, and all the troops joined in, singing the lyrics, "We'll hang Jeff Davis to a sour apple tree, we'll hang Jeff Davis to a sour apple tree, we'll hang Jeff Davis to a sour apple tree, as we go marching on..."

The Rebels played "Dixie" in response. Then the Union band played "Just Before the Battle, Mother" with the lyrics: "...I am thinking most of you...comrades brave around me lying, filled with thoughts of home and God...For well they know that on the morrow, some will sleep beneath the sod... Farewell, Mother, you may never press me to your heart again. But, oh you'll not forget me, Mother, if I'm numbered with the slain."

All the troops stood up and joined in singing on both sides—all except the four hundred Fourteenth US Colored soldiers who remained out of sight. They huddled down in the trenches, fearing that Nathan Bedford Forrest was commanding a unit in Hood's army. The massacre of black troops at Fort Pillow by Forrest's regiment, after the black soldiers surrendered with a white flag and weapons down, was foremost in their minds. This impromptu and unspoken truce was between whites. The presence of black troops struck a nerve in southern troops. Common sense said to stay out of sight.

Ellwood wondered why that song was so popular. It seemed like a sappy, sentimental song that would be avoided by troops about to go in battle. The song had been intended to remind the Rebel troops, even though they outnumbered the Union troops, that they would be charging in the open. They would be facing cannon and rifle fire from troops who were protected by trenches and a berm of earth and spiked logs. Usually the Union troops were in that position.

Ellwood wasn't singing, but Jasper Smith stood by his side, bellowing out the verses from memory. In spite of the music, Ellwood could not help but think that this could be the end. Just last week he caught himself wishing they would see some real fighting—a big battle like Gettysburg. When it was a distant wish, it seemed so gallant and heroic. Now with the bands playing, it seemed dreamlike with a "this can't be happening" feeling. He was both scared and euphoric. Fear and excitement rushed through him. He was not a man to show his emotions, but he had a hard time suppressing an urge to yell at the top of his voice. But he had to appear in control in front of his company. On the outside he just looked impassive, but on the inside he was churning. Some of the troops were getting wet eyed, and both sides were standing in full view of each other with their weapons at rest position. Should he do something? What if it was a trick, and the Rebels opened fire with them standing out of the trenches?

Seeing the effect on the men and fearful they might throw down their arms and join together, a Confederate office shouted, "Play 'Dixie' again." The sadness of the moment was replaced by Rebel yells and shouting. The sound was overwhelming, as it seemed all thirty-five thousand Confederates joined in the singing.

"Play 'The Battle Hymn of the Republic,'" commanded a Union officer. The band let go with all the volume it could muster.

"Mine eyes have seen the glory of the coming of the Lord. He is tramping out the vintage where the grapes of rather are stored. He hath loosed the lightning of his terrible swift sword," the Federal troops sang especially loud, "His Truth is marching on. Glory, Glory, Hallelujah…His truth is marching on."

"Get your men off the roof!" a Confederate officer shouted. "We are going to start shooting." The band stopped playing and quickly descended. They swapped their musical instruments for weapons and dove into the trenches.

A few "pop pops" escalated into a blind-firing spasm with mini balls bouncing off the bank walls and kicking up dirt in front of the trenches. No one was hit as everyone had time to get under cover. Even with all the firing, the mood was somehow festive. Some, to be playful, stuck their hats on sticks and pushed them up over the trenches. The hats were quickly ripped to shreds by gunfire, causing uproarious laughter in the Union trenches.

Fool Me Once—Shame on Me

The Fourteenth US Colored had not seen battle. All from Tennessee, the unit had only recently been formed. Their white colonel, Thomas Jefferson Morgan, was a West Pointer with considerable combat experience. They waited with loaded rifles, not firing but holding back, for they feared the Confederate charge over the trenches was coming. The white troops' old muzzle-loading rifles took some time to reload. It did not occur to them that the wild firing left them temporarily unarmed after each round. The attack never came that day. With darkness, the firing stopped. The Union troops had unlimited ammunition, and the Confederates were clearly conserving theirs after the initial round of firing.

As night turned the wet air to dark, the rapid radiation of a cloudless, night sky created a cooling effect. The nearby river generated heavy fog, and it was hard to see six feet in front of your face. This would be the second night of waiting.

On the first day of fighting, the Union troops comported themselves well. Then numbering about 1,800 troops, they drove off every attempt to overrun them. When the Confederates tried to convince them to surrender and invited them to survey the Confederate troops under a flag of truce, Colonel Doolittle refused. Less than a month earlier, the white commander of another US colored unit, that was guarding the rail line twenty miles north, had been tricked into thinking he was vastly outnumbered. Nathan Bedford Forrest had paraded his troops in a circle, and the fort surrendered. Members of the Eighteenth Michigan and an Ohio regiment had rushed up reinforcements on a train, and even though far outnumbered, they had fought to within yards of the fort. They were cut down by fire from all sides, even from the fort, which then raised the Confederate flag. Only eighteen men and officers of the three hundred Union reinforcements escaped death or capture. Ellwood was one of those. Posted to protect the rear with a detachment of men, he had seen the Rebel flag hoisted and the main unit shot down. He and his few remaining men rushed back to the train, which steamed furiously to Decatur, to report to Colonel Doolittle. As Captain Weatherhead, the commander of Company K of the Eighteenth Michigan, was taken prisoner, Ellwood was promoted to a second lieutenant and became the acting commander. His main strength was administration, and with his excellent handwriting, he was well suited to write the endless reports and inventories required by regulations.

Forrest released some of the captured Eighteenth, as he had no way to transport all captured troops to the South while operating behind Union lines. He had to travel quickly and lightly. The released Union soldiers reported the trickery of Nathan Bedford Forrest, and the premature surrender of the fort was considered a disgrace. Most of the troops in the fort were black and had begged the commander not to surrender. Their fate at the hands of Forrest and his men, who particularly hated black Union soldiers, was unknown. But naturally, they feared the worst. None of the black troops were among the released Union soldiers, and if they were still alive, they had, at best, been returned to slavery.

So, when General Hood tried to show Colonel Doolittle the hopeless position of the fort, the colonel would not listen. His telegraph to Huntsville got action. General Granger returned in a rush with a trainload of federal troops, who filed across the bridge to bring the strength to five thousand. When it became apparent Hood was not bluffing and he actually had thirty-five thousand troops, some of the junior officers wanted to retreat north across the bridge and destroy it. General Granger would not listen. Defending the fort, at any cost, was exactly what Generals Grant and Sherman wanted. This little fort had bogged down Hood's entire army, and Nashville was buying time to build its defenses even more. The fort was a sacrificial lamb. In fact it had been established on the south side of the Tennessee River as an apparent offensive threat to the rest of Alabama. Its purpose was to thus hold Forrest in check so he could not help stop Sherman's march through Georgia.

The month before, fearful for the safety of the fort, then-commanding General Stevens had wired Sherman that he needed reinforcements. His men were untested militia, not regular army, and the cannons were too few and worn out. The fort could not defend itself, let alone mount an offensive attack further south. General Sherman had responded by sending the Fourteenth US Colored. General Stevens promptly resigned. General Granger, a regular army officer, took his place. General Granger understood the strategy and was not about to surrender. It would be a fight to the death or capture of every man.

"There will be no surrender," Granger said with absolute finality. No one doubted it. Unlike the regulars, the volunteers often spoke up and participated in the decisions with considerable debate. Not this time. In a sense, they were almost prisoners of the fort with only the narrow pontoon bridge across the river as an escape route.

Ellwood was prepared to fight, but these units volunteered for the war under the impression that in ninety days they would whip the insurgent southern rabble. They had not, in any way, intended to march into the valley of death. Now, two years later, they were going to be slaughtered for the greater good.

One Dead Man

Ellwood had never shot anyone, at least not where he could directly observe the results. Whether or not some of his shots had connected in previous skirmishes, he would never know. He shivered in the cold as the fog thickened. Thousands of soldiers, Ellwood included, had to relieve themselves in the trench as the dark and fog could get a man lost just walking two feet. It was not only cold, but it stank. At night, there was no way to get food or water either. Everyone was confined to the trench.

The sound of someone stumbling in the night confirmed that walking about was impossible. The stumbling figure fell over the barricade into the trench right in front of him. His startled voice was clearly southern.

"What outfit this?" he asked.

Ellwood could just see the outline of a figure. The dim lantern revealed a Confederate hat. Ellwood was pulling his saber when a soldier next to him raised his weapon and fired at the Rebel point blank. The man fell down in the mud and gurgled briefly.

"Breach in the line. Fire at will!" Ellwood tried to shout, but the words came out strangled, strained. He was soft spoken by nature and did not often raise his voice. His voice did not carry, even under the best of conditions. An unknown figure, standing next to him repeated Ellwood's command.

"BREACH IN THE LINE. FIRE AT WILL!" the voice boomed out—echoing, amplifying Ellwood's command. From the sound of the voice, it was clearly a Fourteenth colored soldier.

Muzzle flashes lit the trenches and further confirmed the Confederate uniform on the corpse at the bottom of the trench. He had no shoes and was thin, very thin—a boy, more a boy than a man. If it were a Confederate sneak attack under the cover of night, there would be a lot of dead bodies out there. No one returned fire. Apparently, it was just a lost teenager, probably looking for a place to pee or trying to find his guard post. The involuntary bowel movement of the dead man/boy really stunk up the place, but there was nothing that could be done until daybreak. Ellwood began to talk to his new partner from the Fourteenth.

"Thanks for the assist."

"I mean no disrespect—I, I didn't know you an officer. Our officer does not stay wit us in the trenches—I got just excited and..." the other voice replied low and deliberate with a note of concern.

"Oh hell!" said Jasper, who was about two feet away. "Ell's just a dirt farmer like me, only he has straps on his shoulder because he can write up reports and such. I'm Corporal Smith, Eighteenth Michigan and friend of his royal highness the lieutenant here." Some chuckling sounded around them.

"Pay no attention to Jasper," Ellwood replied. "He has a hard time taking orders from anyone, let alone someone he grew up with, who now is his lord and commander." More chuckling came from the trenches.

"Throw him in the stockade, Lieutenant!" came another voice. It was Squire Morrison, another Eighteenth volunteer.

"We're in the stockade now," replied Jasper.

"That's for sure," came a chorus of voices.

"What's your name?" asked Ellwood.

"Sergeant Emory, Fourteenth Colored."

"What are you doing here?" asked Ellwood.

"My captain order me, report to him up in headquarters with a how we do'in report, and I got lost in the fog. I just standing here real quiet, figuring I sound more South than North. If I talk, you might done to me what I done to him. When Johnny Reb fell in here, I knew right off from his voice he from the other side. You boys talk real different."

Ellwood was very curious and wanted to talk. Even though he had enlisted to end slavery, he had not personally known any colored—"darkies," as Grandmother would have said. He had been taught that all were created equal in God's sight and that it was evil to do what the South was doing. Although he had to admit that his experience of them, so far, made him fairly detest the race. He had seen them as civilians in Nashville, and they were noisy and boisterous. Their children were mouthy; their men fought. Ellwood had been raised to be quiet when around adults and to be respectful of them. He expected children to be that way around him. He was also raised to resolve disputes by talking, and if that failed, he was supposed to let higher authorities, like parents or judges, decide. Fighting was condemned. Singing was not condoned. The Quaker prayer meetings were silent events where a person could speak his conscience, but only did so infrequently. Hard work and self-reliance were required. Most of the time the Quakers spent alone or just with immediate family. Most of the farm community kept to themselves and only infrequently came together as a group, such as going to church, a funeral, or a wedding. Here the blacks hung around in noisy groups. He just avoided them as much as he could. In fact, this was the first time he had talked to an Ethiopian, as they were sometimes referred to in polite society.

The sun rose and burned off the fog. Ellwood saw his new partner for the first time. He looked up. Both he and Jasper were five foot, six inches tall and weighed about 140 pounds. The sergeant was a head higher and a good deal heavier. Ellwood also could see the dead soldier clearly now. Suddenly he felt very sorry for the boy and his family. He was so thin, and his uniform worn out. His feet were bare and crusted from marching without shoes. He was just a poor dirt farmer who got caught in the war fever that swept the country like some disease, spreading from person to person. For a brief moment, Ellwood wanted to believe the night could be relived, and this time the man would be captured, not killed. Nausea swept into his innards. But in an instant, he snapped back. The reality of it hit him. This war was gruesome. He was not a man to let his emotions control him, but now he just wanted to go home to the farm—see his family—and just forget these past days.

The Devil Is in the Details

Ellwood wanted to talk, but he knew he had to go brief the General's staff. With the fog lifting, another full-frontal attack seemed imminent. Everyone else's spirits were high in anticipation, and with daylight, hot coffee and biscuits appeared for the men in the trenches. General Granger knew many battles were lost just from lack of something to eat or drink, and much effort had been put into preparing and distributing food and drink. Protected by the bank building, a large cook tent gave off the smell of coffee and bacon. With the railroad at their back doorstep, the troops were well provisioned. Psychologically, the smell of food and coffee drifting over to the Confederate side should also have a demoralizing effect.

Ellwood exited the trench via a sloping cut in the back, which allowed safe passage to the headquarters building. He took his coffee; a plate of eggs with bacon, biscuits, and potatoes; and a dish of oatmeal with big lumps of brown sugar. He felt somewhat guilty, as he had spent the war up to this point eating equally with his friends. His promotion to an officer had now set him apart.

"Who gave the command to fire in the dark?" asked Colonel Doolittle.

"I did, sir. We had a Rebel come over the trench, and we thought..."

"Can he talk? Bring him in for interrogation now," commanded General Granger.

"Well, he is dead. He came right in on top of us, and we just..." Ellwood swallowed the coffee. He was parched and hungry.

"Good, that's what you're supposed to do," General Granger cut in. Ellwood looked at his sleeve and then glanced down his front. He had mud and blood dried on his uniform.

"Expect a full attack just as soon as the boys on the other side have had time to shit and eat a bite," General Granger continued.

"From the looks of the dead man," Ellwood interrupted the general, "they don't have a bite to eat."

"Then they won't need to shit," someone else exclaimed.

"Well, this one was saving a shit for his last pleasure," Ellwood responded.

Some laughter broke out, but the rest of the room froze in tension, particularly among the senior officers who would never interrupt a general.

"That's good observation," Colonel Doolittle tried to rescue Ellwood. "If this one is starved, then likely most of them are in the same condition."

General Granger just shook his head, as if to say, *I give up. May this war be over, so I can again command men who just say, "Yes, sir" and "No, sir."* But he continued with newfound patience and even some admiration for men who felt free to speak their minds. "They won't wait long, I figure. Hood has to get across today or move on. Time is not on his side. He's desperate for rations and ammunition—they're coming over with all they got. I know you think we should pull back and blow up the bridge, but that just speeds him to the next crossing point. The longer we tie him down and kill his men, the better for holding Nashville. The election is only eight days away. You let him win, and we lose our president. All the dying at Shiloh, at Gettysburg, at Stone's River, at Lookout Mountain, all the losses everywhere have been in vain. You'll know that all your life. You keep your head, and you lead your troops. Then you can rest knowing that if you don't do anything more in your life, you can still look at the morning sun burning off the haze and appreciate that you weigh heavy on the right side of the scales. You crap your pants now, and it would be better if you died, rather than carry that stink around with you the rest of your days. Sometimes a man has to decide to do the right thing, no matter what, than to do the wrong thing just to live another day. We don't have to die today, but we have to take that chance. Bring home honor to you and your family."

"Colonel Morgan," the general paused and looked for a face.

"Yes, sir," said commander of the Fourteenth Colored.

"General Sherman writes me that he did not think slaves could fight but that they surprised him. He says your men can hold their own and then some. Is that true?"

"Yes, sir. I was with 'em, and they're going home in one of two ways—free and alive or free and dead. But they're not going back to rags and whips. They got 'US' on their uniforms, and they got rifles in their hands. They've been ruined as slaves. You would've seen a sorry sight before they put on the blues. Now you'd think God Almighty had sworn them in, such a change came over them. Yes sir, they can fight. They have fought, and they will fight. Even that devil over there won't prevail—the sea parted, they crossed over, and they are not going back."

There was a stir among the lower-ranking officers. Their worst fears were confirmed. The devil was on the other side—Nathan Bedford Forrest. Better to fight thirty-five thousand troops under Hood than two thousand under Forrest. And this was both. Goodbye, Mother, goodbye.

"Well, I figure Hood to bring up artillery," the General continued. "He's taken over our outer-cannon positions to the east. The positions are aimed the wrong way for him to hit our fort, but he could blow up the bridge, just to cut us off and take our provisions and ammunition. You order the Fourteenth out of the trenches to spike those cannons. We've a gunboat on the river that will pepper the Rebs from the flank, but your boys have got to go up and over. Colonel Morgan, will they do it?"

Hip, Hip Hurrah for the Fourteenth

It was silent. Ellwood was sure every other officer present was also thanking God they were not given that order. Up and over, out of the trench, exposed and charging into enemy cannon with a bayonet, a hammer, and a rattail file! My God! He had heard of such a thing, but that was legend—campfire stories—not something you actually did. They would have to pound the file into the cannon's fuse hole and then break it off with the hammer. That ruined the cannon. But, getting there under a hail of bullets and then sticking the other side with a bayonet before they stuck you—that was the devil.

"Yes, sir," replied the colonel matter-of-factly. "They'll do it."

"All right. The rest of you have to put bullets in the air, as thick as apple blossoms blowing off a tree in a cyclone. Colonel Doolittle, before the Fourteenth goes up and over, you organize a detachment from the Eighteenth Michigan to also go out of the trenches. But slip down low, out of sight by the riverbank, and shoot towards the cannon positions from the side. Gunboats will shell them from the river. Dirt embankments will protect the cannons, so your gunfire won't do much except distract them. When the gunboats stop firing—then everyone stops firing at the Reb cannons—that'll be the signal for the Fourteenth to go up and over to attack them, man against man. Any questions?"

Ellwood led thirty of his troops out, creeping low along the river. The Eighteenth detachment peppered the Rebs then sprinted back, low shielded by the riverbank, back into the fort. Lookouts lying flat upon the bank roof watched the action as three hundred black soldiers poured over the position. The Rebs first simply fled, skedaddled, as the lookout reported later. The Fourteenth spiked the cannons. The Rebs counter attacked, and the Fourteenth, less five dead, ran back to the trenches. After a moment of stunned silence, the white troops let out a "Hip, hip hurrah for the Fourteenth!" For the first time, the black and white troops homogenized. They finally talked to each other, each side straining a bit to understand the other's unfamiliar way of words and sounds.

"Sumthin' goin' on over in Reb land," said one of the lookouts atop the bank and then scampered down the ladder. " A new Reb general it sure looks like." It wasn't Hood. With one arm useless, sleeve pinned up, and a stiff wooden leg, Hood was easy to spot.

"Give me a description," General Granger demanded.

"Well, not Hood. This feller, he got his limbs intact."

"Get me a spyglass." Some of the officers snickered but stopped when Granger cast an eye bolt their way. Ellwood figured the general probably knew all the Reb generals on sight, except for Forrest, because they were all West Pointers like him. Ellwood was right.

"That's General P.G.T. Beauregard," said General Granger, now on top of the roof. He squinted again, "And there's Forrest and four more—can't make them out."

The General slid down the ladder. "Get ready for an all-out attack. P.G.T. Beauregard looks none too happy. Beauregard's just under Lee in command. He and Hood just don't see eye to eye. Hood calls P.G.T. by his rightful name: Pierre Gustave Toutant, just out of disrespect. P.G.T. doesn't like his proper name. But Beauregard means just one thing. Jeff Davis is not too pleased that Hood has been bogged down here three days. Now the whole Union army knows his whereabouts. Beauregard wants this fort today, I think. Why else has he taken command?"

General Granger ordered a sapper unit to blow up the bridge if the Rebs overran the fort. Ellwood's worst fear froze him. Why hadn't they retreated and then blown up the bridge? Were fifty-five and more men dead for nothing?

"General Granger, you need to get back on the roof." One of the other lookouts charged into the room, oblivious that a private was ordering a general. General Granger climbed back up the ladder. The whole Confederate army was forming. It faced the fort with shouldered arms, and then turned left face, marching west in orderly columns and rows. No one fired. They watched, befuddled. A trick?

They were all gone in an hour, and Ellwood then left the fort to wander where they had been. He found nothing to show that thirty-five thousand men had just been bent on killing him. He didn't see much, except some smoldering fires, some mounds covering the freshly buried dead. He was amazed.

The End Is Near

Ellwood paused to admire his penmanship.

Huntsville, Alabama, April 1st, 1865

Dear Mother and Father:

You no doubt read of the fearsome battles back in December up by Nashville. I am sick with killing even if it is those accursed Confederates. Thanks be to the Almighty that I was not in that scuffle directly. We were rushed up but held in reserve. I didn't have to fight. That was a blessing. Reports show as many as twenty thousand of Hood's boys were killed. Our boys had the new repeating rifles and just cut them down. Hood's whole army was nearly wiped out. But that devil Forrest lived and slipped by us. We chased him but lost the scent. We think he and his band crossed back over the Tennessee into Mississippi. But we should be home soon. Show this to Jasper's parents. He doesn't write.

Ell

P.S. The war should be over soon. When we return, a fellow soldier will be staying with us until he can get settled. He's a colored man but you will like him.

Bedford, Michigan, December 24, 1865 — All Is Calm

"Let us end this beautiful Christmas Eve with 'Silent Night' as we pass the flame from candle to candle." The Methodist minister gazed from the pulpit, "And say a silent prayer for all who lost their lives in our terrible tribulation. Thanks be to the Almighty that it is finished."

"Amen," said Jasper and Ellwood, as they passed the flame from candle to candle.

Pulaski, Tennessee, December 24, 1865 -- Kludux Clan

"Pass the bottle around." Five ex-Confederate soldiers lifted a bottle to their lips, swigged, and grimaced. "Wall, we got the name. Kinda' catchy, kludux clan."

"That's 'Ku Klux Klan'—means 'circle of brothers.'" The old general glanced at no one in particular. Then he said, "But, you can call it 'kludux clan' if'n you want. And we're all agree, the best man for Imperial Wizard be Forrest?"

"To Nathan Bedford Forrest!" they all said together.

New Year, Old Thoughts

The date was January 1, 1866. Ellwood sometimes had difficulty believing he was in Michigan. He kept flashing back to Decatur—especially to Nathan Bedford's black son. Sometimes he wondered if he was still in Alabama, and Michigan was an illusion. That walk outside the fort kept recurring in his dreams. And he had kept part of the story a secret, even from Jasper. What could he do? Colonel Doolittle had sworn him to secrecy.

He told part of the story that night in the tent when he swore Jasper to secrecy. But the war was over. Maybe it was time to speak out. His thoughts drifted back to Jasper and Sergeant Emory. He had to remind himself that Sergeant Emory was no longer a sergeant. Now that Emory was living at the farm, it was awkward. Neither could bring themselves to call each other by the first name. It was always Lieutenant Janney and Sergeant Emory. Jasper had no such problem, and those two really hit it off, unlike the rest of the town. They couldn't even take the sergeant to church on Christmas Eve. Well, time would change that, as the town got to see a man, not some idea. Were some of Nathan Bedford Forrest's prejudices alive in Bedford, Michigan?

Prejudice—to pre-judge. No, Forrest had post-judged. He knew blacks were not inferior. He had been a slave trader. He saw them as a threat—knew that talents abounded in them, just like in white folks. Ellwood pondered the day that Hood's army marched on, and Ellwood slipped back into that day once again—as he often did.

Northern Flicker, Purple Martin

Ellwood, satisfied that Hood had hightailed it, decided to walk beyond the protective trenches and walls. The fort, once his protector, now oppressively held him. Five thousand men all jammed together with no room for a hike. He missed walking and trees. The bare, treeless killing zone surrounding the fort stopped at the edge of the woods. The woods waved branchy arms and beckoned. Ellwood planned to walk just to the east where the Fourteenth had spiked the cannons—not too far. But the trees had him. He set a course directly south of the woods.

He savored the solitude, the silence broken only by some raucous crows squabbling over some discarded crumb. It was so reminiscent of the family farm that it felt right.

He breathed shallowly until he walked beyond the stinking latrine trenches that the Rebels had left uncovered—a parting gift. As he approached the line of trees, he could see busy squirrels, waggling bushy tails, chattering an alarm. Small birds flitted branch to branch. Oaks and pines mingled, emitting fresh pine smells with a touch of decaying, oak-leaf musk. He breathed deeply, purging both North and South stench and staleness.

Then directly in front of him arose a commotion. The ground exploded. Startled, his arms flew out—futile prehistoric wings that left him earthbound and momentarily paralyzed. But the wings of the birds in front beat effectively as they lifted up. He snorted as he recognized the bright, white flash on rumps rising from the ground, up and away to the trees.

Northern flickers he recognized right off—unmistakable, black hyphens mingling in scallops among the creamy white feathers. The flicker was a good-sized bird. He would listen, after they settled, for that familiar drumming sound they make by beating a tree with their long, stout beaks—their song. It was Ellwood's kind of song; he felt he and the birds were kindred souls.

The commotion over, other birds tweeted from the trees—an eastern bluebird, purple martins. *Like me,* Ellwood thought, *down south, away from the winter. But unlike me, they chose to come here and can leave any time they want.*

"Sweet, sweet," the purple-martin chorus sang, as if to cheer him up.

A distant, steamy whistle from the railroad across the Tennessee River broke the spell. Suddenly aware it was getting on in the day, Ellwood reversed and strode for the fort. Its security now beckoned. Not a single soul had followed him. Somehow it seemed much further away than it should have been. He picked up the pace. His pistol and saber, now familiar friends, consoled him.

About halfway to the fort, a movement on his left tickled his eye. Turning, he squinted to better focus. A single, tiny figure approached, growing from dog size to horse size. On it came. Now a rider outlined against the gray western horizon. Ellwood searched behind the rider for more. He briefly considered a run for the fort, but he knew a thousand eyes watched him—their old musket rifles still ready. At best he would be laughed at and at worst, shot by his own men.

Was Hood's departure a trick? The lone rider approached. The gray horizon blended but could not hide the gray Confederate uniform on the rider.

Ellwood drew his pistol, cocked the hammer, and pointed it at the figure. Ellwood's arm held the pistol steady; the shakes he had four days ago on Hood's arrival were now gone. The man raised both arms, palms spread. Ellwood stopped. The horse stood still, and then it craned its neck as if asking the rider, "What now?"

"Dismount and keep those arms high," Ellwood commanded.

"I've got to grab the horn, or I will fall. I won't move fast," the man under the gray Confederate hat spoke—low and slow.

"You keep one hand up while you do that," Ellwood said as he looked at the man's face. A Negro. A Negro in a Confederate uniform. Ellwood's brain protested, trying to process this turn of events.

Ellwood just motioned with the pistol toward the fort, and they walked single file, Ellwood at the man's back. He looked up at the fort and saw nothing but rifles all pointed at this figure. Ellwood veered off to one side.

This Confederate was no boy. He was tall like Sergeant Emory. Not thin. Strong. Good boots. Black skin with a wide nose and eyes set well apart. His well-fed horse neighed softly and walked directly behind this Confederate puzzle. The horse was brushed to a beautiful chestnut color.

A detachment of blue uniforms now filed out of the fort, rifles pointed. Someone commanded this surprise soldier to lie down face first. Then the Union Blues removed the man's Confederate hat, the revolver from his holster, and the rifle from the saddle holster. They found a knife tucked in his boot. Removing both boots, they tied his hands behind his back, and several pulled him upright, none too gently—but not violently either. They stared at this black apparition; everyone was mute. Some of the Indiana cavalry came out, muttered admiringly at his horse, and led it to their stables. The chestnut followed willingly, smelling horse on these soldiers.

"Get Colonel Morgan and Sergeant Emory—double quick. Tell Colonel Doolittle what we have here," Ellwood commanded. They all walked into the fort.

Pandemonium Reigns

Once inside the trenches, men milled about, shouting, pushing, and hoping for a better look. Ellwood struggled, finally exiting the trenches with the prisoner, and then marched him to the bank doors. Colonel Morgan, Sergeant Emory, and a detachment of the Fourteenth joined him.

"I think we better take him inside," Colonel Morgan paused, "but wait until I check with the general." General Granger next appeared at the door and surveyed the soldier. He asked for his pistol, which someone produced.

"Where are his boots?" the general inquired of no one in particular. Someone produced them, and the general frowned as he held them.

"Untie him. Put your boots back on. Bring 'em upstairs. Colonel, you and the Sergeant come too. Who brought him in?"

"I did sir," Ellwood answered.

"What the hell were you doing outside the fort," the general said. Not waiting for an answer he wheeled about.

"Follow me." Sergeant Emory hesitated. Colonel Morgan motioned him with a wave, and they filed upstairs.

"Get some coffee for everyone." The general looked at the prisoner. "Are you hungry?" Without waiting for an answer, the general ordered biscuits and johnnycakes for everyone.

"Sit down," the General said, sitting at the head of a highly polished, long maple table that had close, wavy grains. Big, comfortable chairs waited. An orderly brought out some fine china cups and saucers.

Everyone sat, save the two colored soldiers. "No, you sit here and here," the general waved at seats on both sides of him. Both colonels moved one seat down to make room. Ellwood sat at the far end. Other senior officers filled the void.

"Bring me his weapons," the general ordered, looking at the soldier's empty holster and sergeant stripes. "Are you cavalry?" Usually only officers and cavalry carried revolvers in the Union army.

Ellwood sat silently observing as the general first examined the revolver, a fine-looking Colt Model 1860, .44 caliber. Ellwood carried a newer but smaller Colt Model 1861 Navy, .36 caliber—lighter and better for a foot solder. The mystery soldier's gun was a repeating rifle, the Maynard Carbine, .52 caliber. Both weapons were far better than the old musket rifles the Fourteenth carried. The general and Colonel Morgan began an interrogation that lasted well into the night, and weariness descended over everyone.

When Ellwood emerged from the building, a crowd of soldiers was waiting for him. Someone had started a small fire to sit around—outside, behind the trenches. He was tired, but he knew he couldn't sleep until he gave them some facts to chew on.

"He's from Nathan Bedford Forrest's personal guard—one of Forrest's slaves. About eight of 'em, along with fifty or so white soldiers, form a guard around Forrest. He always rides with 'em. They got the best weapons, food, and horses," Ellwood told the men.

"Bedford and Hood are fighting amongst themselves," he continued. "Old West Pointer Hood, he doesn't cotton to Forrest—the man can't read or write. But we know he can fight. It was Forrest's idea to hit us with a surprise attack. He told Hood it's the only way to get to Nashville by election time. He figured we would be run over easy, and they would get the whole army across the bridge before word got out. They easily lost a thousand men, maybe more, in that first charge.

"Old Bedford knew then that the battle for Nashville was lost. He wanted to go back and try to hook up with Lee in Virginia. Hood was furious that the attack failed—blames Bedford. Hood had his orders to take Nashville, so he kept up the fight here. Would have stayed longer than four days if Beauregard hadn't shown up and ordered him to march west to the shoals, where the river is too shallow for the gunboats and they can wade across. About seventy miles west.

"Why would a slave fight for a slaver? Well, old Bedford promised them freedom if they won the war. They're being told old Abe will lose the election and that McClellan will make a deal, cutting the country in two parts.

"But when they saw the Fourteenth charge out and spike those cannons, it was more than our new recruit could stand. Bedford's not schooled in war. He doesn't know any rule but kill and win. And, Bedford's soldiers don't trust him—they fear him. Bedford lives to kill. Killed men before the war when they crossed him. Killed one of his own lieutenants when he argued with him. All the other white Rebs are real jealous because Bedford's coloreds got the better food, horses, and such. But Bedford trusts them.

"So, when they marched off, four of Bedford's colored guards were sent ahead to scout out a crossing. Our mystery soldier split off and hid till Hood's army passed him by. Then he came back here—figures Forrest won't miss him until tomorrow. He wants to join the Fourteenth Colored, and the colonel was glad to oblige him. There's more, boys," Ellwood finished, "but I'm tired and gonna turn in."

Tent Talk

Jasper and Sergeant Emory poked their heads through the tent flap. Ellwood looked up at them, finding the candle lantern plenty bright, once his eyes adjusted. He put down his quill and paper.

"Writing a letter home," he said. "Sit down. I expect you want some more about this mystery soldier."

"Well, yes. Seems mighty odd that General Granger sat down with him—him with such a fancy horse and those boots." Jasper scratched match to boot, lit his pipe, and started drawing on it until it was glowing. The smoke filled the tent with a pleasant sweetness. He removed a flat flask from his boot, took a swig, and shuddered a little.

"The sergeant, here—like you—doesn't foul his mouth with this stuff," Jasper tucked the bottle back in his boot.

"What do you think, Sergeant Emory? You get a chance to talk to him? You smoke?" Ellwood asked, fumbling around for his own pipe.

"No, sir." The sergeant stood a bit stiffly, as there were only two chairs—both occupied. His head reached the top of the tent. He had to tilt a little. "Seems mighty queer, him bearing a pistol."

"And a fine pistol at that. And he speaks pretty well—has some learning. Like you, sergeant. How do you explain that?" Ellwood asked.

"The missus, sir. I worked in the house, and she didn't cotton to slave talk. Speak proper or out to the field. I learn't real fast. 'Spect it was the same with him."

"Maybe. Sit over yonder on the cot. I'm going to tell you a little secret. But, you don't let on where you heard it. You make a friend of him. Talk to him, and see if he's spinning yarns or talking straight." Ellwood, leaning forward, spoke softer than his normal, soft voice. "He's one of Bedford's sons, he says. Another son—he's riding with Bedford too, but he is white. Both were treated mighty fine, but the white boy was treated finer. And Bedford, he won't call him—our new Negro—his son. The man says Bedford took up with his mother, but he was kept a slave, just treated better than other slaves. He's not the only spawn of Bedford and his slaves, but this slave woman was— is—special. She's sort of another wife. Bedford's white wife's a real-fine, gentle, educated woman, but there's nothing she can do. Everybody in the household knows, but no one dares speak of it. Bedford's a mighty violent man. Kill't many a man before the war—likes to kill us Yankees personally. Even killed one of his own lieutenants when he sassed him. Bedford's mighty rich, a big slave trader. I've heard he's one of the biggest—in Mississippi, or anywhere. And he's so rich that he personally foots the bill to equip and pay his regiment." Ellwood found his pipe and tamped some tobacco down the bowl.

SHEATH THE SWORD

Knapsacks and haversacks were tightly packed with all their belongings, and the regiment formed up in Tennessee for the last time. On this day—June 26, 1865—the Eighteenth was minus more than three hundred souls than when the unit was sworn in on August 26, 1862, in Hillsdale, Michigan. More than three hundred lives had been lost or were missing, and still the Eighteenth Michigan considered itself lucky. Maybe some of those missing would turn up when all the prisoners made it home. They had not yet heard about the *Sultana* tragedy. The riverboat, *Sultana,* churning up the Mississippi with released Union soldiers held in dismal Confederate prisons, had exploded, killing many on board. Many were from the Eighteenth, captured when they surrendered to Forrest.

"DISMISSED," Brevet General Doolittle commanded his remaining seven hundred troops, and, by his own words, he became banker Doolittle about to board the train. The north-bound train, chuffing, switching, and tacking, finally stopped at Jackson, Michigan. The troops had spent five days and nights sitting on the rocking, clacking trains, interrupted only by welcome walking to necessary transfers.

Corporal Jasper, Lieutenant Ellwood, and Nathan Bedford Forrest's son banded together on adjoining seats, ignoring glances from other white troops. All wore uniforms, but Forrest's son had a new name and a new uniform. His papers listed him as Sergeant Craft, Fourteenth US Colored—a lie.

Jasper and Ellwood chattered loudly, excited that they were home bound, back to their farms, back to their families and friends. Back to normal. Sergeant Craft sat silently. Even though he was a free man, he was off to a strange land where no farm, family, or friends waited to welcome and cherish him.

"How'll we get to our homes?" Jasper wondered aloud.

"Oh, we should be able to rent a rig to get to Bedford. Then you can borrow one of our horses to ride to your farm," Ellwood responded.

"Bedford?" Sergeant Craft stiffened.

"Seems a bit strange, doesn't it? But that's my home—Bedford, Michigan. Nothing to do with your father, I tell you," Ellwood paused—horrified he had said that. Luckily, the noisy train drowned out his words, and no one seemed to notice.

"Does anybody know we're coming?" Jasper pursued. "I want to sleep in my own bed, eat mother's home-cooked meals, brush down my horse, and ride when and where I want. No more infernal marching, except to the tavern, for sure, for a drink. Maybe tell a few tales." He frowned and repeated his question. "So, does anyone know we're coming?"

"Oh, I sent a telegraph, but there's no way to know if they got it," Ellwood responded, "And I asked father to get a message to your folks, but they must know from the news that everybody is coming home."

"How would your folks get a telegram," Sergeant Craft broke his silence. "Just wondering. I haven't a notion of where I would send a telegram."

"Well, actually I asked Colonel...forgot he's General Doolittle now...to send the telegram to his bank. All the tellers know our family, so when father or one of my relatives goes to the bank, they'll give them the telegram. They'll let my family know, maybe—bet they never got a telegram before." Ellwood smiled at his cleverness.

He then looked at Sergeant Craft who remained silent. It suddenly dawned on Ellwood that Craft was no doubt thinking about family and friends he probably would never see again—reliving a past life he hated beyond words. He was no longer a slave and in charge of his own destiny, but what a different future awaited him. He had no farm to return to, no banker friend of the family—Good Lord, no family, no old friends. Instead, he had a new name, a new identify. Where would he live? What would he work at? Who would hire him? Would there be other black veterans? Would the whites be friendly? How long could he stay with Ellwood? Where would he go after that? Was freedom also fearsome? *These must be thoughts racing through Craft's mind,* Ellwood thought.

Just then the conductor's practiced voice announced, "JACKSON NEXT STOP. EVERYBODY OFF. JACKSON NEXT STOP." The train slowed, then rolled to a banging halt. The blue-capped, blue-uniformed, newly released Union soldiers stared out the car windows. A crowd stared back. The soldiers grabbed their possessions. Ellwood strapped on his sword. He, Emory, Craft, Jasper, and the remaining gaggle of soldiers cautiously descended from the train to the platform. They scanned the crowd with eyes hardened from three years of scanning for those that would kill them.

This crowd stepped back to make room and then cheered the stunned soldiers. Their cheers buffeted the ears of the soldiers, washing away the tedium and tiresome train ride. Faces recognized faces, arms embraced arms, smiles abounded, and tears flowed. The train engine's stack exhaled indifferent sighs of steam and a dirty, misty coal vapor—both mixing with the hot, humid Michigan air. No one noticed the heat or the dirty air. They milled about, excited murmurs mingling with cheers and laughter. Gradually clusters of friends and families took soldiers to horse-drawn wagons and buggies. Those soldiers were not so greeted stood silently watching, waiting, looking.

Ellwood first recognized the team of horses. As they were searching the crowd, a team trotted towards them on the dusty, main road of Jackson. Topsy and Shaggy, the family's workhorses, plodded on their giant hoofs easily pulling a wagon empty, save two men sitting atop the front bench of the wagon. One man was holding the reins and commanding with a parade-quality voice that originated from below the diaphragm, "WHOA!" The horses obeyed.

"FATHER! ROBERT!" Ellwood responded. Robert jumped down, and Father climbed down, looking for the first time at Ellwood in his uniform. He was now three years older with different, piercing eyes. Then they shook hands mightily and firmly. Their hands clasped the tops of their shoulders—no hugging allowed. Then Jasper met the same greeting. Sergeant Craft stood there staring.

Jasper motioned, with a flung out arm, "This here's Sergeants Craft, and Emory, Fourteenth US Colored. And this is Jacob, Ellwood's father, and Robert, his brother." After just the slightest hesitation, the men shook hands but without a shoulder pat.

Robert stared at Ellwood's sword, hanging in its sheath at his side. "Can I see it?" Ellwood grabbed the gold-plated handle, and then stopped. "Let's leave it holstered for now. Wait until we get home." Robert decided without asking that he should make room for Ellwood on the driving bench next to Jacob. Then Robert clambered into the wagon bed with Jasper and Joseph Craft following him. They sprawled on the hay that was softening the wooden wagon bed.

"GIDDYAP!" Jacob commanded, with a flip of the reins. Ellwood sat erect, turning his head to look for familiar faces. The horses peered straight ahead—glad to be heading for home.

CONVERSATIONS

"What's the secret part you wouldn't tell me back in Decatur? "Jasper snorted and stared at Ellwood.

"Hmm, well, it's still a secret and will be as long as we live. So don't go shooting off your mouth when you swallow a few glasses of whisky," Ellwood stared back.

"But here goes. Bedford's son didn't just decide to switch over to us at Decatur. He had been sneaking messages before Hood hit Decatur. That's why General Granger had us in the trenches waiting. He knew Hood was approaching."

"How'd he do that?" Jasper now leaned forward, as Ellwood had lowered his voice, even though there was no one within earshot.

"I only know some details—not all—but he would write out a message and find a colored family nearby when they camped for the night."

"He can write?" Jasper sat up.

"Better'n you, that's for sure," Ellwood went on. "So he would tell this colored family if they wanted to be free they better get this message across the river and find a Union soldier. Then tell him to get this to his commander—this from the devil Forrest's den. All the top officers were told that any message from the devil's den had got to be sent by fast courier—not telegraph—to the Huntsville command."

"How would they know it was not a fake?" Jasper looked puzzled.

"He had a code name, signed the message with the name 'Venir Vidi.'"

"Venir Vidi? What kind of name is that? And why not by telegraph? And anybody could sign that name if they got hold a letter that he was carrying and change the message to fool us." Jasper interrupted.

"Darned if I know about the name, but the graycoats were listening in on all our telegraphs," Ellwood continued. "And he always put an extra period at the end of the second sentence. So if anyone forged the name, they'd most likely miss that little detail."

"So the war's over, why keep it a secret now?"

"General Granger had a long talk with our new friend, and he was sure that Forrest will track him down, no matter how long the war is over. Forrest plans to keep up the war against the colored, even after the war. He is going to do it by a secret bunch of thugs, pretending to be only concerned about Confederate veterans being treated proper after the war. They plan to keep slavery alive by another name and beat, kill, or torture any colored that dares live like a free man. They want to strike terror in the new, freed slaves so they still submit. Bedford's a master at putting on one good face to the ladies and gentlefolk and the very face of a demon to the colored. It's part hatred and part fear. Bedford knows that the colored are smarter than anyone realizes because he was so close to them as a slave trader. He's a vicious man but highly cunning and full of deception.

"So our man was given a new name, which he will carry the rest of his life. No one can know that Bedford's son still lives."

"So Craft is not real name? What's his new name? He's not staying with you anymore. So can't you trust me?" Jasper's face formed into a pout.

"Don't know and don't want to know."

"Won't he be safe here in the North?" Jasper half-asked himself. Then he answered himself, "Nope, there are plenty of folks here that will have no truck with colored, especially if they see them as a threat."

"All I know he is going to study law somewhere. Did you know Colonel Givens of the 102nd Ohio is a judge in Ohio? Anyway, he and the general talked about that on the day that Bedford's son showed up. They didn't know that I could hear everything at the end of the table. The ceiling had a dome, and whoever sat at that end could hear a whisper at the other end. I bet the chairman of the bank use to sit there during meetings."

"So I bet you know his new name, after all," Jasper smiled, tipped his head back, and looked down his nose. "Venir Vidid, that's just plumb stupid."

AUTUMN OF 1888

"Can't believe it's been twenty-three years since the war ended. I should've keep in touch. I was surprised to get your letter. Well, it didn't surprise me too much. Well, not too much. No, well, I was really surprised. But when the Children's Blizzard hit in January out West, and then the Great White Hurricane hit back East in March, I said this year has got a bad spirit to it. And then this in September... Well, when I got your letter I said this doesn't surprise me—not too much. After all, it had been a year that had a bad spirit right from the beginning. So yes, I was surprised that Ellwood died. He was a good man—thought he would go on to something in the government or such. Now, if you had died I would have said that you drank too much and were kind of ornery. So that would have not been such a surprise. Say, did Ellwood ever take a drink? You know I am powerful sorry I missed the funeral. I didn't get your letter until after. I expect it was a big one. Do you keep up with the other fellows in the Eighteenth? I haven't been able to find the Fourteenth veterans. We scattered all over. Had no roots to go back too, Well, none that we wanted too, except maybe to shoot the old bastard." Diamond Emory leaned back and poured a shot of rye whiskey down the hatch. He shuddered a little and wiped his mouth with his sleeve.

"Diamond—that your real name? We never called you nothing but Sergeant Emory. Never knew your first name. Diamond? That's it?" Jasper also leaned back and took a shot of the rye. He shuddered a little too. "Don't expect Ellwood would approve of us drinking to his memory."

"No," Diamond leaned forward and put his head down on his hands. "That's what they call me up in Detroit. Made some good money—got a nice business black smithin'. Bought a nice diamond stickpin for my wife, and the name just stuck. After all them southern boys trying to kill us and we make it. And then Ellwood ups and dies. I mean, how old was he?"

"Forty-eight," Jasper nodded. "Never took a drink, so far as I know. Like Lincoln, in that respect. So, what is your actual first name?"

"That would be hard for me. I need a drink now and then. To calm the nervous, if'n you know what I mean. I always go by Diamond. My first name reminds me of when we were bound up. So I let it go. Left it behind in Tennessee. When I enlisted in the Fourteenth, I had to give them a name, so I made it up. Emory. It just came to me like that—Emory, a new name, a new uniform, a new man. Just like that." Diamond leaned back in his chair again and looked at the ceiling.

"So, what first name did you give?" Jasper poured another shot. "You had to have two names in the army."

"Say, what day did Ellwood die?" Diamond leaned back forward.

"September twenty-third, a Sunday."

"A Sunday. Somehow that seems right for a man that never took a drink. You know, back in Tennessee we at least got to have our beliefs. That got us through—most of the time. But no church marriage was allowed. No baptism name. Just bare-bone religion. They couldn't take that from us. They would if they could, though. Sometimes I wake up and fear all this is a dream and I am back in rags in Tennessee. You know that devil Forrest with his KKK is still aiming to keep the colored as slaves. I hear terrible things. Not just the Klan, but also something called the White League and another called the Red Shirts. They're all a bunch of mean, angry, cruel folks, taking out their sins on the people they sinned against. They are regular thugs—not even that manly—cowards hiding under bed sheets. And then this President Hayes took out the army from the South and left these pour souls to fend for themselves against the devil and the devil's helpers. You think we ever going to be truly free?" Sergeant Emory stared from the porch down the lane that led to the house. The trees made a sort of tunnel, and the birds flitted and chirped about. It was crisp but not cold. Mrs. Smith walked out with cups of coffee, and both men took the cups and sipped. Jasper put his full shot glass over on the sill. Both men stared silently for several minutes

"Never allowed marriage? I did not know that. You married now? Did you know Ellwood had ten children—seven boys and three girls. The oldest boy is only seventeen." Jasper picked up his shot of whisky but just held it for a moment. And again he put it down. "I believe if Father Abraham had lived, things would have turned out better. Old Grant he tried, but he was a better general than a president. Still, he did his part—can't expect one man to save the world I guess." Jasper shook his head.

"No, well, I've got to head back to Detroit. Don't want to be out in the dark. My family is expecting me. You ever get up to Detroit, just ask for Diamond's Livery. I got a livery plus the black smith shop," Diamond stood up. "Thanks for the use of the barn."

"Yes, well, sorry we didn't have room in the house. What with all the commotion from the children, you would not have slept much even if we had room."

"Oh, my rig is real comfortable. Felt good sleeping with the horse chomping oats for music."

"Yes, you've fixed up that rig like a little house. A house on wheels," Jasper said.

"That way I can lock myself in, and no one can see a black man sleeping." Diamond took a draining swallow of coffee from the cup.

"It's a long way to Detroit—what thirty miles or so? Maybe stay another day?" Jasper drained his coffee too.

"No, got to get back to business and all. Got a passel of kids too. Just had to come down and pay respects to Ellwood. 'Spect it was a big funeral."

"Oh, yes, full army honors and all. Lots of boys from the old Eighteenth and others were there too. Yes, it was a right proper funeral, the kind a man hopes for." Jasper sat his coffee cup down on the sill and looked at nothing in particular.

"Noticed he was buried in a Methodist cemetery. Was Ellwood not a Quaker anymore?" Diamond swatted a fly from his hat and put it on—a big, blue-brimmed hat that pulled down to his eyes. He tucked in his shirt—a fine black linen cut to fit his frame. He was a big man. He rearranged a small revolver in his boot and pulled his sock up to conceal it. His pants were also cut to fit but with loose legs that came down over the boot—not unlike the Union uniform he used to wear.

"No, the Quakers are real tolerant, unless you marry outside the faith. You know his son married my daughter."

Jasper stood up too. His five-foot, six-inch frame put his head about chest high on Diamond. Jasper also wore a blue shirt, but it was made of cotton and loose fitting. His pants were a bit baggy but comfortable looking. He wore no hat, which revealed his hair had turned white. His full beard was just as white. His fair skin somewhat reddened from the sun. Both men had dark eyes that fixed like a cat about to spring on some unsuspecting critter. Diamond was smooth shaven with hair still largely black. He could have passed for much younger than Jasper.

"Do tell. You mean the lieutenant married someone who was not a Quaker, and they kicked him out?" Diamond stared at a noisy crow being attacked by a Northern Flicker that was patrolling a big oak.

"No, well, he sort of kicked himself out," Jasper continued," Actually, he never joined the church, none close by. But his inside was still Quaker. Warring goes against a Quaker's insides. But then slavery did too. I guess you can't fight yourself too long, so he just drifted away."

"No fighting even to free bodies from tyrants? Why, they sold us like livestock! Wouldn't teach us to read or write. No respect for marriage. Didn't even allow it. Beat us—degraded us to keep us down. Knew full well we were as capable as anyone. But we were just property to them. Money machines. Stripped our children away and sold them with an evil, cold heart. No fighting to stop that?" Diamond stood at full attention, looking at nothing.

"No, expect not. You know I'm not a Quaker. I don't get caught up in that fight. Too complicated—too many high thoughts. I don't have a chance in that scrap," From the porch Jasper gazed down the lane.

Diamond followed his gaze. "You have a proper farm here."

"Yep, born here. 1848.Yes, the soil is good, rich, and black. This whole area was a swamp, and then the government cut in ditches and drained it out. We plant sugar beets and corn. Some hay. Big garden too. Carrots, snapping beans, lima beans, onions. Not many peas, though. It's too hot. But we have squash, cukes, turnips, potatoes, and apple orchard with hives—honey and hard cider in the fall. Real tasty," Jasper smacked his lips.

"Nice team of work horses, too, I noticed," Diamond pushed his hat back." Say, I just remembered one of my horse's shoes is a bit loose. Suppose we could fix that? You being a smith, too—taught me the trade, after all. Who would think a hammer and a nail could make such a difference? A man needs a skill that others need. And I got that now. Now, that is freedom."

"Yes, yes, well, let's go shoe that horse. A couple of mine need checking too," Jasper started for the barn, and Diamond walked alongside him.

"You know, I found that a black man like me with skills provokes some folks into a hate fit. Seems they thought we were beneath them because we only did sweat work. Then, when we show them up, they feel lower than the black man they had created in their mind. Their eyes see the skin that used to cover a slave—a slave that was degraded and whipped into submission. They think the skin caused the condition. But when they see the skills, they fear the world turned upside down." Diamond opened the barn door, and his horses whinnied a welcome and snorted a command to get moving.

"You know, I understand your point better than I want to. I confess that before we got acquainted with the Fourteenth US Colored I might have felt the same way, somewhat. A little. But then that battle gave us all a fair look at the inside.

But I fear without the battle, it's going to be a long time before folks see the person wrapped up in the skin. A long row to hoe. Well, say, that shoe is loose! Let's nail it down. Nails are on the bench over there." Jasper held the hoof, and Diamond hammered it on tight. They harnessed the horses, who stamped impatiently to get a move on. High up in the sky waves of geese flapped their way south on a cool, brisk, north wind.

Diamond hopped on the carriage bench, took the reins, and looked at the geese. "Don't envy them. Not going my way. The only thing I miss is the hills. I never saw such flat land before. You can see your back if you look long enough. Well, good-bye, then. Giddyap!"

Jasper waited until he couldn't see the rig, as it shrank down the tree tunnel that framed the lane out to the road. He walked back to the porch, found his shot glass of whiskey on the ledge, and downed it, rocking away the afternoon.

Any Color as Long as It's Black

The Grand Army of the Republic (GAR) rented the entire hotel to for its annual reunion. By 1915 the Civil War veterans were dwindling fast, and with the advent of World War I, it seemed appropriate to give one last, full measure of honor to this select group. Great anticipation leaped from man to man, as they stood on the dock waiting to board a steamer for the island resort in Lake Erie. Many had heard of the luxury hotel, but few ever imagined they would have a fling there. Rooms went for a scandalous $2.50 a night, but the GAR had convinced the management it would be good public relations to lower the rate. The price for this epic reunion was fifty cents a night, which included three square meals.

Jasper and Sergeant Emory stood patiently waiting on the dock in the orderly line of men.

"Where'd you park your horses?" Jasper asked, his face showing he really did not care—that it was just a safe question to pass the time.

"No horses—got me a Model T Ford. My boys drove me down from Detroit on Telegraph Road," he said, and by the look on Jasper's face, his reply was clearly not expected.

"What? You're driving one of those infernal machines? Why, you're a smith and livery owner! Those confounded, horseless buggies will never take holt. Why, where does the fuel come from? You can't grow it. It stinks, and the discharge is no good. Now, a horse eats hay, which we grow, and then we use the poop to fertilize. And a horse knows its way home, if you have a drink too many and doze off. Tell me, how does the horseless contraption do all that? Why, I won't have one! What about your livery business? Why would you spend good money on a foolish fad like that?" Jasper tipped his head back and shot a glare at his pal, who stood there smiling.

"I sold the blacksmith and livery, and me and my boys own a filling and repair station. Business is real good, and I don't have to shovel poop no more and brush those beasts down. When the barn door is closed, the automobiles don't make a fuss, and they don't eat. I once heard a man say you should never buy anything that eats, and that was good advice. Your horses are eating right now, and my Model T is just sitting there waiting without need for any attention. You got to anticipate the times. Old ways are lost ways." Diamond looked down at Jasper smiling.

"Well, if that don't beat ever. You best remember how to blacksmith because those stinking wells will dry up soon. Think the Model T will run on hay? Now, I grow that, and I understand haying. Don't have any idea how to make gasoline out of filth pumped from the ground. Do you?"

"Nope, don't have to. Old Mr. Rockerfeller takes care of that. No planting and cutting hay or sweating and fighting critters that eat crops. Just have to own a tank and a pump, and the stuff gets delivered." Diamond was about to continue, when he noticed the real frown on Jasper's face. But just then the line moved, as they started boarding the ship. They walked in silence on the gangway up to the ship's deck.

Puddinbay

Black smoke trailed the steamer as it left the dock in Toledo and pushed the waves aside. It was headed out in Lake Erie for Put-in-Bay, or in local dialect, "Puddinbay."

The old soldiers from both Ohio and Michigan crowded the deck, their white-haired heads scanning the lake as the ship distanced the shore. Many had never been on a steamer, or even a boat, before, and most had never been out on the big lake. It was a little choppy, but the wind and waves were not severe. The sky was clear. A little on the green side, the lake contrasted with the blue sky where it met the water at the horizon. They were headed for a reunion of the Union soldiers who had fought the good fight. Even though it was some forty-odd years later, and the faces had shrunk and shriveled, the spirit of the warriors had not only been preserved but had also improved with age. Time had called many old comrades to the grave, but those that still stood savored the moment, knowing that it may be the last time for such celebration.

Jasper and Diamond stood side by side on the rail and stared outward silently, with a studied gaze at this new world. Even though it was at their doorstep, they had never experienced it before. Diamond had adopted a new first name—Emerald. He said it fit a man his age better and went with his last name. The old soldiers of the Eighteenth Michigan had shortened it to Emery. "Emery Emory," they said, chuckling.

When they arrived at Put-in-Bay, they met a string of horse-drawn carriages, which took them to the biggest hotel the soldiers had ever seen. The planners of the reunion of these Civil War veterans had chosen well. It was an elegant vacation hotel with over six hundred rooms, a vast dining room, and huge, porch verandas.

After they had settled in their rooms, they gathered at a stand that dispensed liquid refreshments on the veranda that overlooked the lake. They had not seen each other in over twenty-five years.

"Was a little afraid I might have trouble with a room. The fellow at the desk hesitated a little, then just looked at my old Union army cap, and left the key on the counter. Had to carry my own bag though. The only time I fit in with white folks is when I am around the Eighteenth. They see my eyes, not my skin. Wish it always like that. But it's getting better. The Quakers are starting to see me as a man, not just a colored man they have to take pity on." Emory pointed to a ship passing by the island, and all waved.

Tremble at the Sight of the Lord

"What're you doing with Quakers?" Jasper shifted his gaze from the passing boat to Emory.

"Oh, I'm a Quaker now too. Took up the religion. Saw the light. No more war. Besides, I learned the Quakers pushed for abolition, and even before that, they pushed for education, treating us coloreds like we were people, not some kind of two-legged livestock. I still sneak in a Baptist meeting, now and then, to revive the spirit. But I like the silent meetings of the Quakers. I can hear myself think. Don't need no preacher man to connect me to the Almighty. I guess I have always thought that, but I didn't know I thought that, until I heard it said. Then the thought just grew and grew, and one day I set out to find some Quakers up in Detroit. And sure enough, though I was a stranger—and a black stranger, at that—they welcomed me."

"But I thought you couldn't see how the Quakers couldn't not fight in the Civil War?" Jasper pondered his own words. "Should have fought...you know what I meant to say. Thought I had seen everything—you a Quaker. Why, next thing, you'll be pushing for women to vote. Doesn't that beat all? Now, this war in Europe—don't you think that's a fight we should put a dog in?"

"That's the clincher for me. Bunch of kings and dukes and czars sending men like they were toy soldiers and not seeing they're flesh and blood. And for what? Some old geezer got killed, and all the king's men can't be satisfied to just punish the killer. Who's insane, the kings or the killer? I kind of feel a little to blame—done so much talking about the Grand Army of the Republic that my boys kind of got the war fever. They don't see the gore just hear the glory side. Hard to keep them at home when they expect to see a great adventure. Which I got to admit it was."

"A Quaker. Expect Ellwood's sitting up in his grave, saying, 'Well, I didn't figure on that.'" Jasper and Emery both laughed.

"You remember the son of that devil Forrest? Well, he's a Quaker too. Or was. He passed away. Was a lawyer went back down south and helped his fellow man as best he could. Now *there's* a fight we should get a dog in—not with guns but with the truth. Bunch of soldiers that lost a war and taking out their sorrows on defenseless souls. Do you know that old Hood was so ashamed he was whipped at Decatur by a tiny force of Colored soldiers and Midwest militia that he tried to ignore it? All old Hood said was 'tough nut to crack.' He ignored that he lost of passel of men. And tipped his hat. Let General Thomas know that Hood was not hoodwinking him. Now there's a general that never got the credit due him. Like us. You know, if we had not stopped Hood, he might have taken Nashville? If that happened, Lincoln might have lost the election. Then that pip-squeak, McClellan, would have been president and let slavery live on. Think about that. Guess we best enjoy that quietly. No fame like the boys that fought over there at Gettysburg. Of course, I'd rather be alive than famous. But a little recognition wouldn't hurt."

"How do you know all this?" Jasper eyes opened widely, even in the bright sun. "You know his real name? I never even knew that. 'Spect he told you when you both stayed with Ellwood right after the war. Or did he leave before you got there? He came with us, but you showed up later. Then you both lived with Ellwood for a spell, right? But then he left first, I believe. My memory has gotten rusty. Ellwood took that secret to the grave. He would have told me if he knew that he wouldn't not timely go. Or go too early. You know what I'm trying to say."

"Oh, I knew all along. We shared many a story under Ellwood's hospitality. That was a godsend. Don't know what we would have done. No family or farm like you to go back to. But he left first, and then we wrote back and forth. He studied law—old Colonel Givens went back to judging in Ohio and found a colored lawyer that apprenticed him. War of words. He kept up the fight by lawyering. That's the future. Not warring with guns. Words. They are the bullets. Can't hide the truth if true men can speak."

Revelations

Jasper stood silent and appeared to ponder that. Then he nodded in agreement and spoke, "Say, did we ever mention that before Decatur we were in Nashville on provost duty? The Eighteenth had to police the brothels. That was something I tell you. You know those ladies were real pretty and wore such perfume. I can still smell it."

Emery tore off his hat and threw his head back. "You *and* Ellwood? Do tell," he said, and they went off to dinner in the grand ballroom.

20988491R00045

Made in the USA
Lexington, KY
26 February 2013